With a Joyful Noise
Christian Music Resources

I0168207

REFLECTIONS
of the Cross

ARRANGED BY AMANDA TERO

Cover design and formatting by Amanda Tero

Contents

Note from the Arranger

Reflections of the Cross was a beautiful project to work on. What better way to spend the day than to reflect on what my Savior has done for me—by laying down His life in my stead, taking my sins with Him to the cross, and covering me with His blood. I got an immense blessing saturating myself with these songs that point to my Redeemer, and it is my sincere prayer that everyone who plays and listens to them will find the same blessing and be reminded of our Savior's love which took Him to the cross. If you have not yet received Jesus Christ as your Savior, His arms are wide open, ready to forgive you your sins and embrace you as His own.

Greater love hath no man than this,
that a man lay down his life for his friends. (John 15:13)

For God so loved the world, that he gave his only begotten Son,
that whosoever believeth in him should not perish,
but have everlasting life. (John 3:16)

Amanda Tero

Check out **www.withajoyfulnoise.com**
for more arrangements by Amanda Tero.

The Old Rugged Cross

George Bennard
Arr. by Amanda Tero

The Old Rugged Cross

The Old Rugged Cross

The Old Rugged Cross

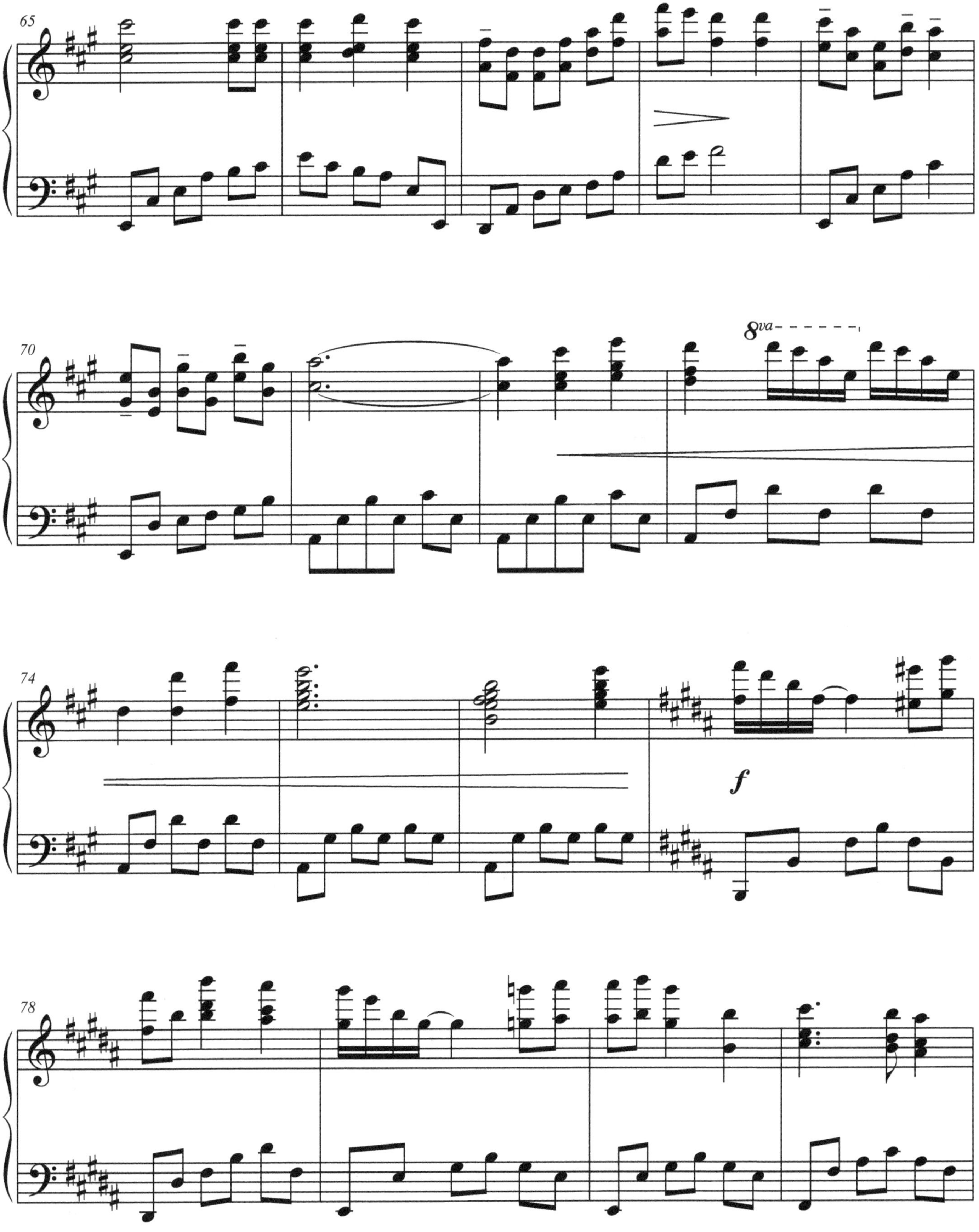
65
70
8va
74
f
78

The Old Rugged Cross

The Old Rugged Cross

At the Cross

Ralph E. Hudson
Arr. by Amanda Tero

At the Cross

At the Cross

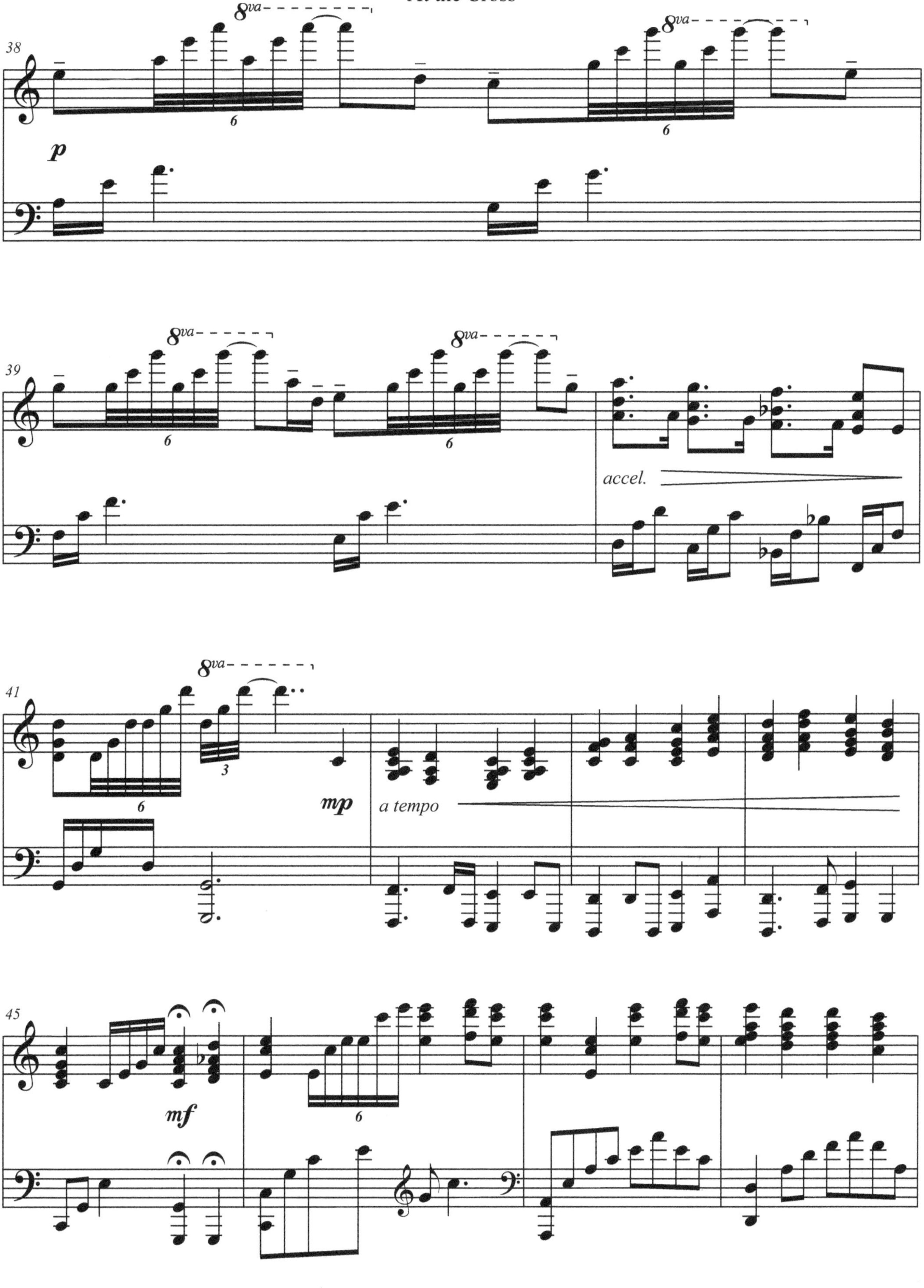
38
8va
6
p
39
accel.
41
3
mp
a tempo
45
mf

At the Cross

When I Survey

Lowell Mason
Arr. by Amanda Tero

When I Survey

When I Survey

When I Survey

When I Survey

When I Survey

O Sacred Head, Now Wounded

Hans Leo Hassler
Arr. by Amanda Tero

O Sacred Head, Now Wounded

O Sacred Head, Now Wounded

O Sacred Head, Now Wounded

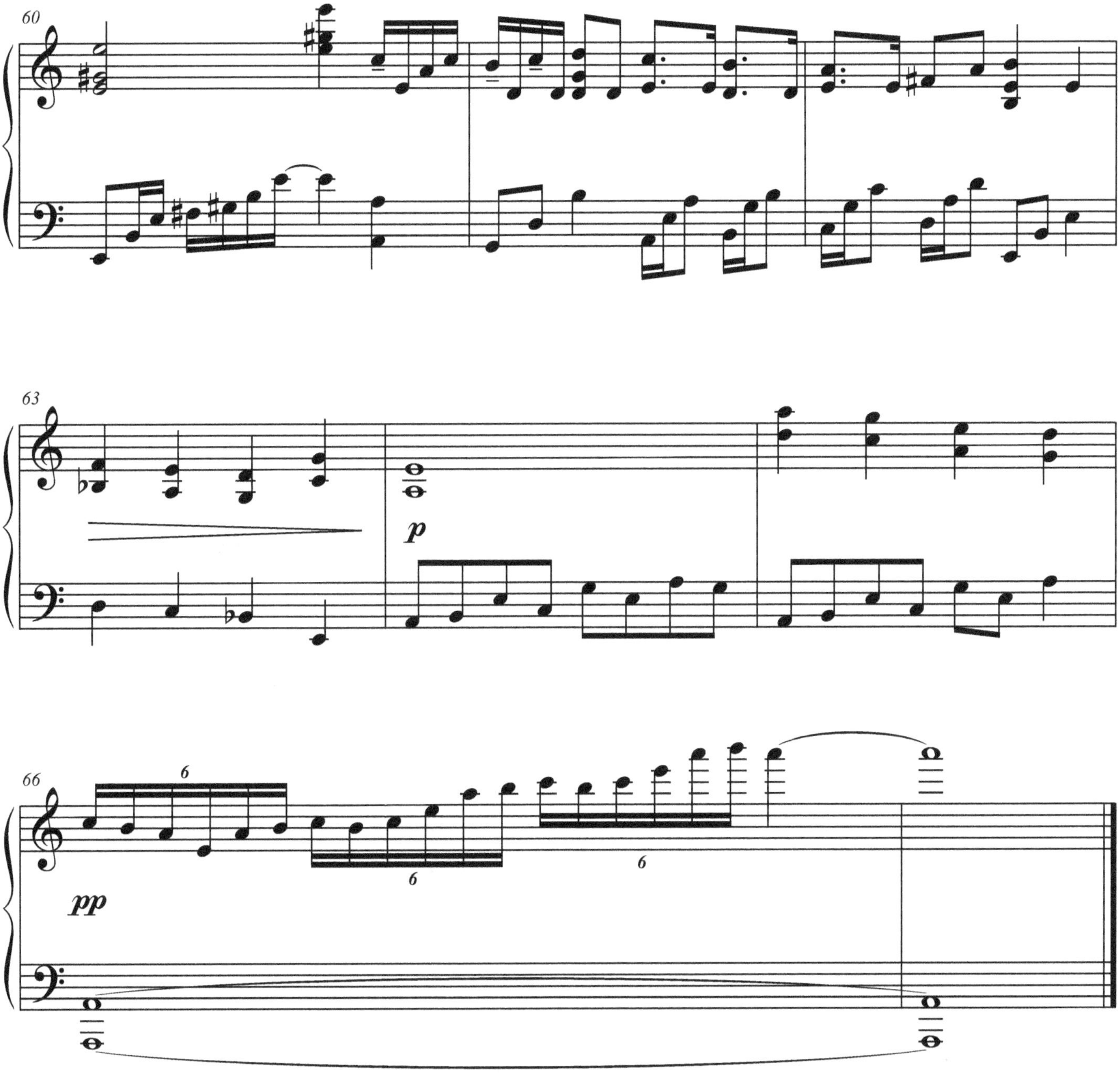
60
63
p
66
6
6
6
pp

Beneath the Cross of Jesus

Elizabeth C. Clephane
Arr. by Amanda Tero

Beneath the Cross of Jesus

Beneath the Cross of Jesus

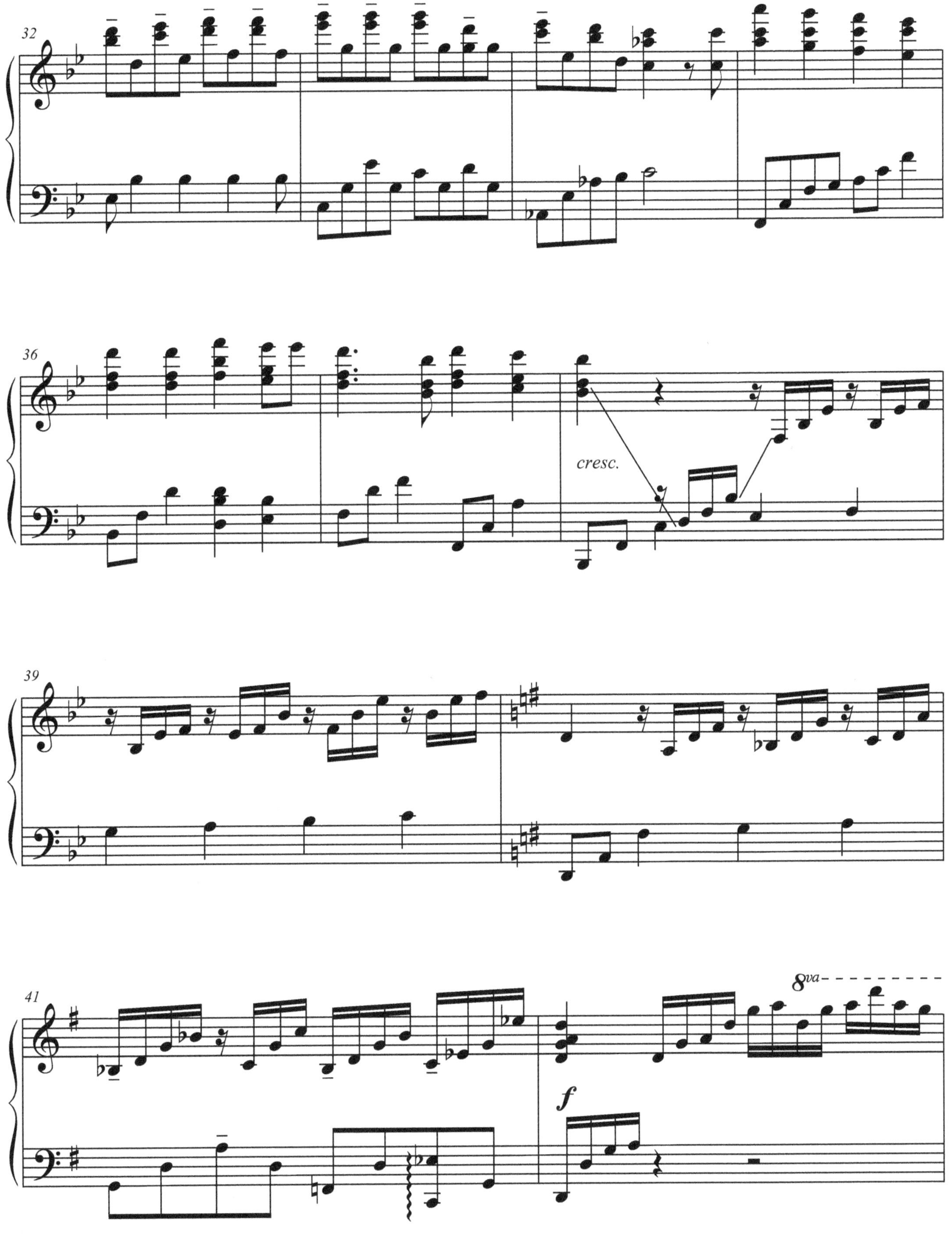
32
36
cresc.
39
41
8va
f

Beneath the Cross of Jesus

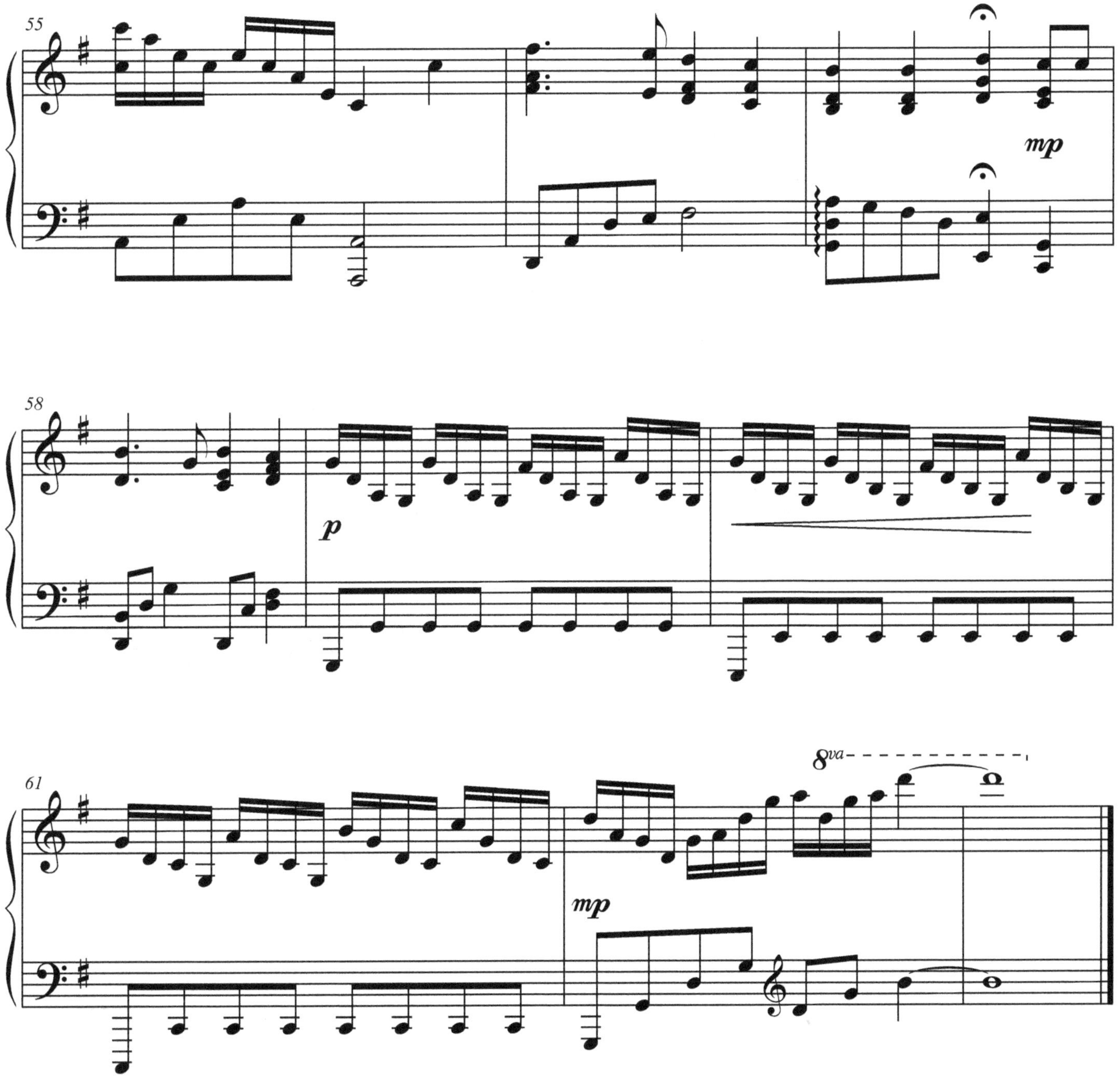
55
mp
58
p
61
mp
8va

I Stand Amazed in the Presence
(My Savior's Love)

Charles H. Gabriel
Arr. by Amanda Tero

With much expression, rubato

I Stand Amazed in the Presence

I Stand Amazed in the Presence

I Stand Amazed in the Presence

Hallelujah! What a Savior

Phillip P. Bliss, Amanda Tero
Arr. by Amanda Tero

Hallelujah! What a Savior

Hallelujah! What a Savior

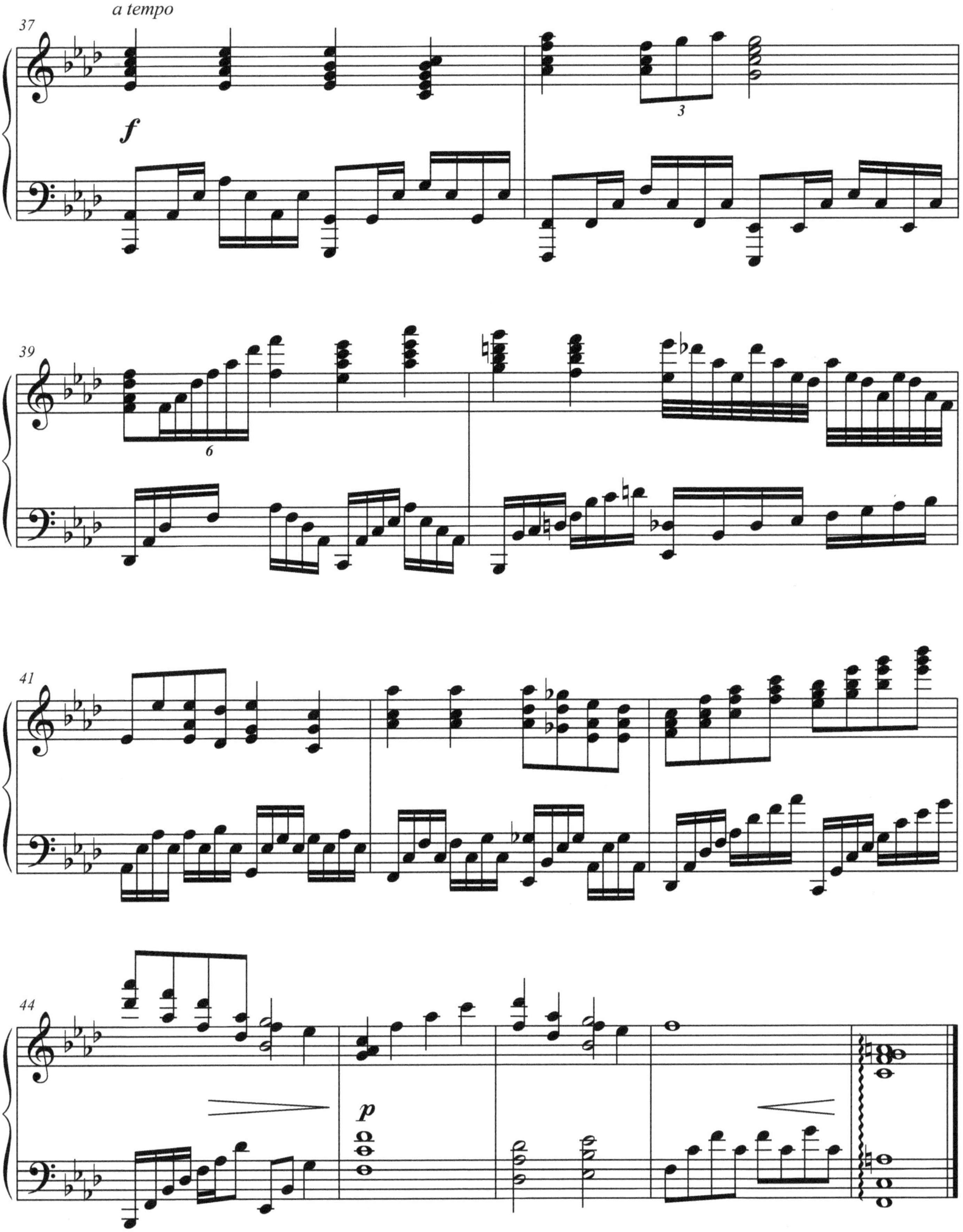
a tempo
37
f
3
39
6
41
44
p

At Calvary

Daniel B. Towner
Arr. by Amanda Tero

At Calvary

At Calvary

At Calvary

At Calvary

At Calvary

Down at the Cross
(Glory to His Name)

John Stockman
Arr. by Amanda Tero

Down at the Cross

Down at the Cross

Down at the Cross

Down at the Cross

Near the Cross

William H. Doane
Arr. by Amanda Tero

Near the Cross

Near the Cross

Near the Cross

Near the Cross

www.ingramcontent.com/pod-product-compliance
Lightning Source LLC
Chambersburg PA
CBHW081241090426
42738CB00016B/3368